# THE SEED OF RACE

# THE SEED OF RACE:

## AN ESSAY ON INDIAN EDUCATION

SIR JOHN GEORGE WOODROFFE

GYAN

*Published by*

Gyan Publishing House
5, Ansari Road
Daryaganj, New Delhi-110002
Phone: 011-47034999, 9811692060
E-mail: books@gyanbooks.com

*Distribution Network*
gyanbooks.com
India, USA, Canada, UK, Australia



ISBN: 978-93-6920-011-5 (PB)

First Published, 1919

2nd Impression 2025

*Printed at:* Gyan Press, Delhi.



**THE SEED OF RACE**
Author: SIR JOHN GEORGE WOODROFFE

# THE SEED OF RACE:

## AN ESSAY ON INDIAN EDUCATION

BY

SIR JOHN WOODROFFE

GANESH & CO. MADRAS

1919

# THE SEED OF RACE

## AN ESSAY ON INDIAN EDUCATION

IN the discussions, now happily current, as regards the nature of, and necessity for, the preservation of racial culture in India, and the nature of the education which should be given towards that end, it is necessary to understand quite clearly what is meant by the term Racial Soul. For if this is understood we have the key to the settlement of the dispute between those extreme Conservatives who would maintain the *status quo* in all respects, those extreme Radicals who would subvert Hindu civilization and substitute for it European institutions and culture, and those who, following a middle path, recognise both the necessity of adaptation to present circumstances and needs, and of basing such adaptation on cultural principles which have come down from a remote past. A great deal of confusion exists, because the nature of the Racial Soul and the meaning of the phrase "maintenance of racial culture" is not understood. Indian philosophy supplies us with some principles which make this matter very clear.

Racial Soul is the Soul either of a particular individual of what is called a Race, or of the collectivity of the individuals who constitute that Race. The first is in Sanskrit (which supplies us with so many useful terms) the Vyashti and the second the Samashti Soul.

Then what is "Soul," to use the English term? According to Hindu notions, so clear cut and meaningful, what is called (often vaguely enough) "Soul" in English is in Sanskrit subtle body (Sûkshma-deha). Each Jîva is

Spirit that is Âtmâ or Shiva, and Shakti, or the Power of Shiva, as mind (Antahkarana) and body (Sthûla-deha). The gross body (Sthûla-deha) is composed of the compounds of the Bhûta or sensible matter. The subtle body is all else than this. According to Vedânta the Sûkshma Deha is the "17", namely, the Antahkarana or mind as Buddhi and Manas (including Ahangkâra), the ten senses (Indriyas), and the five forms of vital force (Prâna). The Sânkhyans include, instead of the Prâna Pentad, the five Tanmâtras or forms of supersensible matter. For practical purposes therefore we may describe the Soul or Subtle Body as the mental or psychical body, and the gross body as the material body of sensible matter (Annamayakosha). Both of these are creative projections of the Causal Body (Kâranadeha or Paradeha as the Shaiva-Shâktas call it) which is the Brahman in Its aspect as the cause of the subtle or mental (Sûkshma Deha), and gross or material bodies (Sthûla Deha).

This causal body (Kârana Deha) is thus the Seed (Bîja) of the other two bodies in which it is manifested. The collective (Samashti) causal body (Kârana Deha) is the seed of the totality of the minds and bodies of a Race and the individual (Vyashti) causal body is the seed of the particular member of that Race.

What then for our purposes is the nature of that seed (Bîja)? This is the individual or collective Sangskâra. At creation (Srishti) Îshvara, by His will, lets the Seed or Sangskâras which inhere in His Power, as material cause (Mâyâ Shakti) ripen, and the hidden Seed manifests itself as Mind and Body, the vehicle of Spirit as an individual (Jîvâtmâ).

What again is Sangskâra? It is the impression upon, and tendency of, the mind, produced by previous action (Karma) and which again in its turn generates Karma. It inheres during dissolution in the Mâyâ Shakti of Îshvara, though latent as cosmic memory. At creation this becomes patent, that is, arises in the mind of Îshvara as the memory of the past universes. Through His will there is a going forth or realizing of it as Mind and Matter. But there are many currents in the outward flow. Any particular racial consciousness is thus a particular defined stream in the whole Cosmic Flow. A particular part of the general Cosmic Memory realises itself as a Race with its beliefs, practices, and social institutions.

Now what is of main importance is the Essence or Sangskâra, and not the particular and transient forms with which it is vested—in short, the General Memory or Spirit of the race, the fundamental characteristics and outlook on life which distinguishes the people of one race from all others. In this Sangskâra or Seed is held the Type of Race of which the individuals are the variational forms. Thus we find in any particular Race some who, by reason of purity of stock or intensity of soul, represent better than others the spirit of Race. So we say of a man that he is a typical

Englishman. Again, the beliefs, practices and institutions of a Race vary during the course of Its History. Nothing is absolutely stable and lasting but the Supreme Brahman Itself. This is due to changes in time, place and circumstance, and in the racial consciousness itself. This is recognised in various ways in Brâhmanism in its doctrine of cycle (Kalpa), four ages (Yuga), Yugadharma, Lokâchâra and Desha, Kâla, Pâlva or time, place and object. The nature of this Cycle is one which requires investigation. Whether it be a mere cycle, or a cycle combined with an upward movement, such as is shown by the spiral, need not be here discussed. It is sufficient to note that variation due to time, place, and circumstance exists. But undoubtedly, so long as a Race exists as a body of men with certain defined characteristics, there is throughout its historical development an element, namely, the Spirit of the Race, which *persists* throughout all the varying forms in which it clothes itself.

This Spirit is a manifestation of the Essence of National Character, namely, the collective Sangskâra. Brâhmanism accepts the doctrine of Re-incarnation but the principles of education here advocated may also be justified upon the Western theory of Heredity.

Now what we must do is to distinguish between the Seed of Race latent as Sangskâra, patent as general national character, and the particular cultural forms which it produces. The former more constantly endures ; the latter more constantly change under the influence of time and other conditions affecting the Race. Where the evolution of the Race is slow it may well be that the forms of a preceding generation are adopted in the present with little or no change. Where however the evolution becomes rapid, due to internal or external causes, a question then arises which demands an urgent answer, namely, whether these forms should be preserved, modified (and in what way), or destroyed. This is the state of matters now when, owing to English rule, English education, and Western influence in general, the question presses for solution whether the Indian people should retain what is called orthodox belief and practice, whether these should be modified to meet new social and economic ideas and conditions, or whether Indian civilization should not be, to a greater or less extent, scraped as out of date.

It is quite clear to me what the answer should be, though the particular application in any case of the principle stated may be the subject of discussion. I would say that we should look primarily *not to the produced* but to the *producer*, not to transient forms but to the lasting Racial Spirit moulded through the ages of which spirit they are the embodiment; not to past cultural forms, which may or may not be applicable to present needs, but to the Spirit of the Race which manifested in them. Thus the Indian Spirit may, in the 10th century, have produced new, or maintained inherited forms.

True conservatism however is not necessarily bound up with the maintenance in the twentieth century of forms a thousand years old, but with the maintenance in its purity of the Racial Spirit which produced or adopted certain forms in the 10th century, and which will produce, if necessary, other new forms or modification of ancient forms to-day. After all it is the general Spirit and Principle which counts. The strictly orthodox may be alarmed at this statement, but they may, in large part (that is as to essentials) rest assured. For if the ancient spirit is conserved, that is if the Racial Sangskâra is maintained, such modification and even apparent novelty as are produced must be, from the nature of the case, in true relation and conformity with the Sangskâra out of which they have arisen. In other words an Indian soul can never for any length of time wander far from the essentials of its inherited civilization.

But what of the extreme Westernizer in

theory and practice? Have we not here a breach with tradition and a new Karma? Will not this Karma generate a new Sangskâra? Certainly there is a breach and a new Karma but that it can generate a Sangskâra which can altogether overpower, in the general body, that accumulated in countless past ages I do not believe to be possible. This assumes of course that the present people continue as an independent racial unity and do not disappear either through disease, intermingling with other stocks or, according to Hindu ideas, pass away upon the rebirth of Indian Souls in other bodies and of other Souls in Indian bodies. The persistence of racial characteristics and what is described as the "call of the blood" is observed in even highly unfavourable surroundings. Temporarily, however, the Racial Sangskâra (though not lost) may be submerged. That is what has happened in some cases through Western Influences in the India of to-day.

In referring to Race, the natural question is —what race? Commonly we speak of the Aryan race. But nobody knows with certainty who were the peoples to whom this term is applied. Aryan is not properly a term of race at all, but refers to a common language and culture spoken by, and belonging to, a group of individuals or peoples. The fact that people speak the same language does not necessarily show unity of race. We hear of some Aryans who, like the English and other northern races were "fair skinned with auburn hair" (Shukla-varna, pinggala-kesha) but these even at an early date had become so rare that they were spoken of as belonging to another Kalpa. Then there were Aryas who were swarthy. But whoever the so-called Aryans were at the date of their immigration into India, it is clear that a large number of the Indian people are not (and probably none are) of pure Aryan descent, though some are purer than others. The dark colour and features of many of the people to-day are evidence of this. There are "black Brâhmanas" and "fair Shûdras" which are considered inauspicious types. In the natural course of things the "Aryans" must have mingled with the pre-Vedic peoples inhabiting the peninsula. Caste has throughout been a preservative institution as regards the higher stock, but caste has not always been rigidly observed and was loosened, where it was not destroyed, during the predominance of Buddhism. Like other peoples the modern Hindus are in varying degree of mixed stock. India however has suffered from such mixture more than some other races, as for instance the English, because in the latter case the mixture was of kindred stocks of fairly equal value, whilst in this country there have been and still are both high and very low stocks. One has only to look at a fair high caste Brâhmana and a Dhangar. This fact is overlooked by European critics of the caste system. So far as the physical features of race are concerned, there is not in England much, if indeed any, difference between a member of the lowest social classes and the highest. And so individuals rise from the first to the second and again fall again. But in India the difference between a high class Brâhmana and a Dhangar is the difference which exists between races far removed. India contains all type of culture extending almost from the neolithic to the present age. Probably this juxtaposition and, in cases, admixture of high and low types, is one of the main, if not the chief material cause, of the arrested development and degeneracy of this country, which has made it for centuries a prey to any one who desired it. The racial tangle is such that one hesitates to base conclusions on it. We are however on surer grounds when we proceed on the basis of culture. There is no doubt that there was a specific Aryan culture (Arya-dharma), whatever may have been the race of those whose culture it was. In its essential definition "Hinduism" or "Brâhmanism," the developed product of the Arya or Vaidika Dharma, is not merely a specific "religion" but a particular culture. This Culture was spread throughout India and affected in varying degrees the Avaidik peoples. But the original Arya Dharma was itself affected. For this reason "Hinduism" as it exists to-day is not the Arya Dharma as it was known in early ages. Thus, to take the instance of religion, the original Aryas had neither temples nor images. What critical and informed person looking at the images of Kâlî, Târâ, Chhinnamastâ can imagine them to be in their origin Aryan concepts. Many "sooty superstitions," as an English writer has called them, have their origin in the black races of India.

For my present purpose, however, there is no need to go back to origins. Kâlî may have been a deified princess of the black Vindhyan or other tribes, and her garland of white heads may have been those of the Aryans. Brahmanism however took this concept and others into its system. Her image stands as the symbol for advanced concepts which would have been incomprehensible to Her original worshippers. Thus her "severed heads" are the fifty letters (Varna). And so with other matters. Thus several races and cultures have gone to the production of the Aryan body and soul as they now exist. The Seed of Race to-day is thus the Indian Sangskâra which has produced the minds and bodies of the Indian people of our time, amongst whom some are rejecting their Dharma as a whole, others are rejecting only what they deem to be corrupt accretion with a view to recover essential principle, and others again are adhering with a firm and sometimes fanatic devotion to everything which they have received from their fathers. The middle path is here, as in so many other cases, the best. For it is the path of evolution whilst the first is an attempt at revolution with little chance of present success, and the last is an endeavour to crystallise for all future time what is itself the product of ages of change. Like however the middle path it is a manifestation of the Racial Spirit. The first, in so far as it professes to reject the Arya Dharma in principle and detail, is a tendency away from it. Vital people require no counsel as to the direction they should take. Being themselves they take it. For this reason a counsel to English people to be themselves would seem to be rather absurdly out of place. Here, however, the circumstances are different. Whilst the present position and its conflicting tendencies may puzzle some, the point really resolves itself into the negative counsel to avoid mere imitation, to be oneself, and to thus enter on the path of evolution which is natural. The call in fact is to be vital, true to oneself and thus in harmony with Nature. In short, the call is for the maintenance of those elements of the Aryan culture which have value. This does not spell any static attitude, which is in fact not possible, but natural development of the Racial Spirit or the product of Aryan culture by assimilation of foreign stuff, if necessary, as opposed to mere imitativeness and automatism, the signs of feebleness and lack of vitality. What in fact is produced by the independent Racial Spirit is another matter with which I am not here concerned beyond saying that it is not necessary and not likely that it will merely reiterate the past.

Now education means to "educe" or "bring forth" what is within the child. We cannot bring forth that which is not there, though it is possible to superimpose something from without. Such acquisition however is not natural or lasting. True education, in the case of an Indian, is therefore the bringing forth of the Indian Sangskâra. A senior member of the Indian Educational Service, to whom I shall later also refer, has criticised this and other statements of mine in a note which I submitted to the University Commission by the observation that according to this principle the child of a Thug should be brought up to Thuggi and the child of a member of a criminal tribe should be brought up to be a thief. Such criticism is considerably below the average of intelligence which we are entitled to expect from a member of such a Service. Probably in every man there are some bad elements. Education does not mean the fostering of these, but of the good elements of character. Evil elements are eliminated by appeal to, and encouragement of, those which are good. In Indian education, as it exists to-day, the matter of first importance is to give the inherited Sangskâra a full, free, play. It will then, with some guidance, develop itself rightly. This means that the primary process is a *negative* one, that is the clearing away of all the foreign incongruous stuff, which is piled over and choking the Sangskâra, as it were a mass of mixed earth and rubbish thrown upon a young shooting plant. Clear this away and let the plant grow.

The next stage of the process is a *positive* one. Nourish the plant properly.

English education has in the past threatened to smother the Indian Sangskâra. Because I have stated this and advocated a system which should give it freedom, some absurd opinions have been attributed to me. I have been thus represented by this critic and some others as a reactionary who would throw back the land into mediæval " darkness," who would exclude all knowledge of the English language and Western science, and as holding that the English education given has been wholly bad, and so forth. On the contrary I have repeatedly said that English education has had some good, as well as some evil, results. The knowledge of the English language, which is that of a vast and increasing part of the world, and of Western science, is essential to the progress of this country, and only one who was either without sense, or an enemy of its advancement, could hold otherwise.

The case which I desire to put forward for consideration is this:—There is the Racial Sangskâra or Seed of Race. Education is the bringing forth of, and giving free development to, this. How may this best be done? In the first case we must consider the *instrument* by which education is given. At present the education is generally a Western education given by Englishmen or English-educated Indians, whose outlook is often more an endeavour to follow that of their own teachers—the English, than the outlook of their own people; that is, the education is substantially an education by aliens. I have said elsewhere (what has been said before me) that there are in some respects probably no two persons more dissimilar than a Hindu and an Englishman. A similar observation has been made by that acute thinker Professor Lowes Dickinson. The educational expert to whom I have referred has given his opinion that such a statement could not either be sanely or honestly held. It is possible that others may not share my opinion, but I think that few Englishmen resident in India will be found amongst them. But of those who disagree with what I say, I would ask the following question. If the two peoples are alike in their character, mode of thinking, habits and so forth, why do not the English people associate socially with them as they do amongst themselves? Why, even when the Indian is English-educated and follows the English mode of life, is he not admitted to English Clubs? The members of such clubs have every right to be exclusive, and I have no sympathy with those who attempt to force their company on those who do not want it; but is it not obvious that the reason of this exclusiveness is to be found in the fact that the characteristics and ways of life of the two races are different. We need not discuss whether the one or the other race is superior. I believe that no Race is superior to another in everything. It is sufficient to say that they are different. That there are also points of cultural similarity I think. If this were not so, English Literature would not be appreciated as it is.

Are the English then altogether disqualified from teaching the Indian youth ? Of course not. To begin with there is the case of the expert. His knowledge entitles him to teach. And it is advantageous to use his knowledge, of whatever race, nation or creed he may be. Then there is the teaching of the English language and of Western culture, its philosophy, literature, art and so forth. This will not ordinarily be better done by an Indian, to whom such culture is as alien as is that of India to the Englishman. Perhaps some will have the conceit to think otherwise. Only the other day I heard of a Bengali saying that he did not speak English like the English because the latter did not know how to pronounce their own language. With however Indian self-development and an increasing knowledge of

European thought and ways, the English teacher may be gradually dispensed with, unless where, being a technical expert of higher attainments than can be found in this country, his services are necessary. On the other hand Indian culture can best be taught by Indians provided that they themselves have a knowledge of, and respect for, it. If they are mere copies of the English, the latter as the original and stronger character, are vastly to be preferred. What however is required are true educationists and not the bureaucratic type, self-conscious of being "officials," or the (generally vulgar) missionary of Imperialism. We live in an age of advertisement, of publicity boards and the like. But bagmen's methods should have no place in education. What is desired is an increase in the number of Indians who can give what is called nowadays a "national education."

Knowledge is not the property of any people. Whether the term "national" be appropriate or not, what is meant is an education suited to the needs of the Indian people. The facts of science may be taught by any. The personal or racial equation enters very little, if at all, into the matter here. As I have said elsewhere, two and two make four in India as in Europe. But racial qualifications do very largely enter into the question of the competency to teach Indian religion, philosophy, literature and art. It is natural that an Indian should best appreciate what his race has produced. It is this side of culture which has been neglected in the education hitherto given to Indian youth. Further, the purely objective sciences must be studied with reference to Indian questions. Thus, it is not enough to study Economics from English Text-books based on English conditions. The fact of Indian life must be considered. These *prima facie* are best known and understood by the people who take part in that life. It seems to me obvious that a qualified and properly educated Indian teacher will better understand his boys, than the best of English teachers are likely to do.

Then, again, in the giving of education, the local conditions should be considered more than at present. Let me give an example which was recently related to me. In a village school the boys were taught in the early hours of the day—a natural time for a hot climate. This was objected to on the ground that teaching should be between (if I remember rightly) 10 o'clock and 3 o'clock, at any rate during the middle and in the hottest hours of the day. It was pointed out that this is not a good time for small children to work. Further, it was not possible for them to take food and drink to their fathers in the fields. The objection was overruled with the result that the boys could not attend. Again brick and mortar is considered necessary for education in this country. There must be pucca buildings with tables, benches, blackboards and what-not.

Why? Because that is the European way. Of old, and even to-day, children are taught in the open air (as is the modern fashion in some places in Europe) under the wide-spreading Indian trees. It is sometimes said that there is not enough money in this country to give education. Why then make it still more difficult by requiring expensive accessories? For centuries a simple and even advanced education has been given without them. It is not chairs, tables and P.W.D. buildings which give knowledge. If pucca buildings and the rest can be given, well and good. Give them. If not, give knowledge without them, under the conditions with which for hundreds of years this country is familiar. In all cases let us go, not according to the artificial departmental rules, but practically according to actual needs and means.

To sum up therefore, the charge of education should be increasingly placed in the hands of the *right type* of Indian. And by this I mean a man who has knowledge of, and reverence for, his civilization and will carry it forward with devotion to truth and the needs of living men and women. Otherwise the right type of Englishman is better.

The next question is, *what should be taught?* The answer to this depends on what is considered valuable. If English culture is alone such, then it alone should be taught, and it can be taught best by English men and women. If Indian culture has value, it also should be taught to Indians by Indians. This is the whole gist of the matter. Is Indian culture to be neglected as in the past, as something without value, or is it to take a place with English studies? It would be absurd to wholly exclude these last. But it is unnatural and injurious to wholly neglect the cultural inheritance of the people whose education is in question. I have been charged with holding the ridiculous opinion that science should be excluded. I must therefore be excused from platitude in saying that science is of primary importance and must be taught. And so also the English language and culture must be taught, both on account of their own intrinsic importance, and of the fact that the English are the Rulers of this country and one of the foremost, if not the foremost, power in the world, which Power is also a great centre of culture. It would be useless to say anything on a matter so plain, were it not for the fact that there are a class of persons who are ready to think that any one who has a word to say in favour of Indian culture, and the necessity for the maintenance of racial character, thereby condemns all foreign cultures, and is endeavouring to foster some system of racial segregation. As I have elsewhere said, all separatism is becoming increasingly difficult, having regard to the form of present world-development. Knowledge belongs to the world and not to any one people, and the more the Indian people know of the rest of the world and its thoughts, the better for them, provided that what is taken in can be assimilated, that is, adopted without prejudice to the individuality of the Indian organism.

The point before us is however a very different one. It is not whether the English language and culture should be taught, but whether the Indian culture should be neglected. This has been the case in the past. It should be given co-ordinate rank. We all know how little value was attached to any thing Indian by Macaulay, the protagonist of English culture, and many, perhaps most, have since then shared, though sometimes in tempered form, his views. Such have regarded Indian religion as a false superstition, Indian philosophy as antiquated guess-work without present value, Indian art and literature as crude and grotesque, its science "seas of butter and oceans of milk" and so on. The young Indian has been subjected to such a strong and continuous *suggestion* of his inferiority, that it is a wonder that any spirit of self-assertion has at all survived. He has been told that he has had no glorious past, that the history of his country is lacking in great personalities, that the "progressive" West is superior to the "immobile" East and its old-world civilization and so forth, and that therefore his only chance of making himself the equal of Western peoples is by giving up his "Barbarism" (as a recent English author has called it) and making himself as like his civilized Western teachers and rulers as possible. If day in and day out, suggestions of his innate inferiority are made to a boy, and the superiority of a foreign civilization is affirmed, he will, according to every probability, come to depreciate his own people and culture. This is what has happened and the racial Sangskâra has been veiled. These suggestions can, and should be, countered by others based on an accurate appreciation of the Indian character and its cultural achievements. The seed of Race will then commence to sprout and flower. When racial character is re-established, *an autonomous centre of receptivity is established* capable of receiving (without risk of being overwhelmed thereby) every form of foreign culture. This is possible because there is then a healthy organism capable of assimilating every form of food presented to it. A knowledge of foreign life and thought is as essential to India as a knowledge of what is its own. It is this last which has been neglected.

One of the extraordinary features of a section of Indian public opinion on this point is the difficulty which some seem to have in understanding what "national" education is. How, it is said, can knowledge be "national?" It is true that the teaching of objective facts is not affected by considerations of Race. There is not, for instance, an Indian and European Science of Biology. Biology or any other science is the same whether in East or West, and may be taught as well by an Indian or European, provided that either know their business. But there are forms of culture into which a strong subjective or otherwise peculiar element enters. Of these one of the more salient examples is Art. We legitimately speak of Greek Art, Japanese Art, Indian Art and so forth. Literature, Religion and Philosophy are other instances. History again is supposed to be a record of objective facts. But one would need to be a child to accept the record as altogether, or even largely, veracious. It is a record not only of some true facts but also of racial, national, and credal prejudices and untruths. "Don't read me History" said the sick Walpole to his companion. "I know it to be lies." But even if we assume history to be all truth, it is obvious that certain portions of history concern one people more than another. In India for instance, in the past at any rate, attention has been given to the history of the English and Mogul occupation, the student being left in ignorance of the happenings of the specifically Hindu period. As regards literature again, it is doubtless necessary for the student of English to know Shakespeare and other great poets and prose authors. On the other hand he should know more of his literature than a few Cantos of Raghuvangsha or the like. Years ago (I do not know whether it is so now) Flint's "Theism" was prescribed for undergraduates, with entire neglect of the Indian treatment of the subject, as if it were unknown to this country and its literature. Even to-day, as H. E. the Governor of Bengal pointed out, students of philosophy learn the Western systems first before their own, and so on and so forth. Government is not alone responsible for this. A considerable number of persons who claim political equality with the English are earnest to dissociate themselves from Indian "superstition" and "barbarism", and to show that there is nothing in their past to warrant their present claims and hopes for the future. Of superstition it is not easy to give more than a formal description: but taking the term in the sense in which these people use it, superstition is to be found everywhere. But a belief is not superstitious because it is of the East, any more than it is well-founded because it bears the import stamp of the West.

If however the Indian people have done nothing which was of value in the past, what is the warrant for supposing that they will ever do anything in the future? Is not the place of those who merely imitate the English, not on the seat of equality with the latter, but as humble disciples at the feet of their Guru. Some think it clever that the weak should imitate the strong. There is however always the risk that in imitating others we cease to be and lose ourselves. It is curious to find some professing not to understand what the movement for national education means. The least intellectual Englishman will at once understand what is meant by the phrase "to bring up one's boy like an Englishman." I am aware of the possibility that with the evolution of man many differences which now divide may disappear. I am as much opposed as any one else to Nationalism on its hind legs anywhere. My hope is the Confraternity of Men. I believe however in the possibility of the friendly co-existence of differing cultural characteristics, and that before India can fully express the more universal culture, which some believe the future may show, She must first realise, in its purity, or recover where it has been lost, Her Self. To deny this is to deny to Her civilization any intrinsic value. The Seed of Race must be first *disencumbered* of all which impedes its development and then *fostered* by an education suitable both as to its *instruments* and *subject matter*. The disencumbrance of which I speak, refers not only to foreign impediments but also the decaying products of the past growth of this Seed. It is not the product of past ages which *as such* has to be maintained or reproduced. It may in fact be maintained if it is good. We are all concerned with the present and the maintenance of the *Seed of Race.* If this be free and strong, it will develop into a plant which will live, that is, a plant suitable to the time, place and circumstance under which it grows: for nothing can live which does not fulfil these conditions. It may be that the Racial Spirit will in some respects reproduce what it has produced before. It may be that, nourished in part by the food of a new and Western civilization, it may reproduce subject to certain modifications, or may put forth some entirely new developments. What is produced is immaterial provided that it is the issue of the freely developing Seed of Race. It must be *free* to develop as it will. Essential alone is the maintenance of the Seed of Race, let it develop howsoever it may. The rightness of the orthodox upholder of the Sanâtana Dharma consists in his staunch maintenance of the Spirit of his Ancient Race. The rightness of the so-called Reformer consists in his desire to uphold only that which is truly eternal, in a form suited to time, place and circumstance, rejecting what is corrupted, upholding a free development as opposed to a mere mechanical and static continuity. Whether a particular "reformation" is justified, depends on the facts of the case. It is a true expression of the Indian Spirit if it proceeds from it. The wrongness of others consists in the neglect or betrayal of the Racial Spirit, in their attempt to wholly break with the past and their denial of the Racial Self. Nothing can thus persist. For persistence is a present and future rooted in the past. Ultimately we are not concerned with any Race but with the good of men (Nara) at large, the earthly embodiment or likeness of the Divine Nârâyana. The form of these embodiments varies. Dharma is the law of form. The only contribution which India can make to the general human good is one which springs from Her own Mind and Heart and not from that of any other.

It must not be supposed that ill opinions, or justifiable criticism, of the country and its people are those of foreigners only. They may be found amongst Indians themselves who have had an English education, for others have not yet learnt to concern themselves with such matters. Recently one of these has described the Indian people as backward, indolent, in the slough of selfishness and slaves. The State must therefore educate them "imperially" and this will create "spiritual bonds." As "Superstition, erotic sentiment, and fantastic mysticism are the great themes of Oriental poetry, *no Oriental nation would be a loser if it forgot its own tongue and learned English instead.*" The people are "unpractical metaphysicians or selfish cowards or passive slaves." For lofty idealism one must go to England—to London apparently by preference, as it is "the heart and brain" of "our goal and ideal" the railway-named "British-Orient-African commonwealth" of the future. England is the Indians' "spiritual mother." "The Empire cannot develop if the Orientals prefer their barren literature and uninspiring history with its sickening record of Sultans, massacres, slavery, empires, and degeneracy." "The ideals of Oriental life are antiquated." "Nothing in the Orient is greater than English literature and English History." Greek philosophy must be introduced to "undermine superstition in Asia." Then the history of the Roman Empire may be used to show the Indian people that their eyes are in front and not at the back of their heads. Indians must revere England as "their spiritual mother," and Greece as "their spiritual grandmother," whilst as for India she is for the people nothing, not even their great grandmother or aunt. In this way the Empire will advance *via* the "British-Orient-African Commonwealth" to the "Parliament of man" of the poet's dreams. There is doubtless some truth in this writer's criticisms of his countrymen of to-day, particularly as regards the class of lazy, selfish, cowardly and subservient persons of whom he speaks. The great man Svâmî Vivekânanda was himself wont to give such people a whipping of vigorous speech. It was he who wrote of his own people "We are immensely selfish" "Our insincerity is awful; what we want is character." "We want the heart to *feel*." "We have become real earthworms crawling at the feet of everyone who dares to put his foot on us," and many another trenchant denunciation of the cowardice, selfishness and falsities of Indian life to-day.

English literature is amongst the most glorious in the world and breathes the spirit of a free and vitally creative people. Greece too was great, how great only the Western, nursed in her cultural tradition and lover of the Powerful and Beautiful can know. But for Her culture she was indebted in part at least to India. It is however only ignorance which can see nothing in India but superstition. She has produced in the philosophers of Brâhmanism and Buddhism some of the deepest and freest thinkers the world has known, howsoever fallen and imitative may be the minds of many of their descendants to-day. Does not the Mahâbhârata say " There is no Muni who has not an opinion of his own." Notwithstanding some truths, these opinions, if sincere, are, I think, the clearest amongst the articulate expressions of degeneracy which I have come across. The writer outcasts himself from any Motherland. The " spirituality " which calls itself " imperial " is understood in this country for what it is worth. The true brotherhood of men and peoples is spiritual. The true path is, whilst purifying one's country of its defects, to uphold what it possesses of essential greatness; whilst honouring what is great in the present and past Western peoples, not to fail in respect for the land of one's race and birth. Rightly has it been said that when a man loses faith in his own historic past, he cannot have any faith in, and respect for, himself.

Together with the teaching of the so-called higher sciences, a technical, industrial, agricultural, commercial education must be given. There are many who favour this and think that education has hitherto been of too general and literary a character. This in turn has produced a veritable legal pestilence. Let it be noted that efficiency in work was not only valued in actual practice but was enjoined by the old Dharma-shâstras. At present slovenly habits are overcoming the Indian artisans and the present talk amongst some is for a cheap eastern market where anything and everything can be sold regardless of quality. This result in an evil time such as ours is due to the exhausting poverty of the country, which gives neither time to the artisan to perfect his work nor choice to the purchaser of it. The artizan has often to work with bad tools, and bad raw materials both of which he has to borrow. The commercialisation of his craft proceeds apace, because greedy middlemen are anxious to secure the fruits of somebody else's labour at a price which gives to the worker the minimum wage on which existence is possible. Sometimes not even that is offered and the artizan finds it better to till the soil. And so the number of landless labourers has swollen in recent years, having increased, I am told, from 10 to 11 lakhs in 1901 to about 45 lakhs in 1911. If, as is likely, the rate is the same for the subsequent period, then the next census may show something like two crores of landless labourers, descendants of the old and famed artisans of India. This is the class which gets one meal a day and which is the first to fall a victim to the recurrent famines. The subject here touched on is of vital importance and would require a volume. If I have not gone into detail on the subject of scientific and technical education, it is not because I undervalue it, but because in the first place such details may best be dealt with by experts and secondly because the principle for which I contend is generally ignored. What I labour for is the preservation in a regenerated form of the Indian soul and the rejection of all mere imitativeness. This is the root of all questions. If there is success here, then "all else shall be added to you." For here we approach the Springs of Life. All evil is a symptom of some taint at this source. It is no use treating a pathological symptom. One must cure the sick spirit which has produced it.

What I have here and elsewhere contended for is the ancient principle of Svadharma. Such novelty as if there is in the position is due to the fact that recourse is had to an ancient Eastern principle, and not, in the more fashionable way, to one or other of the dozens of modern western theories which jostle one another in their claim for public acceptance to-day. Svadharma, as a counsel, is a bidding to hold to our own. In fact, there is no question of choice in the matter if we would survive. Dharma is the law of all being, and Svadharma is the nature of, and law governing, any particular being in regard to which the term is used. A being which does not act according to its true nature cease to be. Dharma is one of the profoundest concepts which the mind of India has produced. Dharma is worshipful. " Self determination " of which we hear so much to-day is only a limited application in a particular realm-that of politics-of a doctrine which was preached thousands of years ago by Shrî Krishna in the Gîtâ—To understand and follow Dharma, is to have true religion. *What* is Dharma is another question.

This principle of *Svadharma* and its practical application to the various problems of life was, as I have been recently reminded, the constant theme and burden of the message which it was the mission of the great Svâmî Vivekânanda, to deliver to Modern India. Said he: "We have seen that our vigour, our strength, nay, our national life is in our religion. I am not going to discuss now whether it is right or not, whether it is correct or not, whether it is beneficial or not in the long run, to have this vitality in religion, but for good or evil it is there; you cannot get out of it, you have it now and for ever, and you have to stand by it, even if you have not the same faith, that I have, in our religion. You are bound by it, and if you give it up, you are smashed to pieces. That is the life of our race and that must be strengthened. * * That is the national mind, that is the national life-current. Follow it and it leads to glory. Give it up and you die; death will be the only result, annihilation the only effect, the moment you step beyond that life-current. I do not mean to say that other things are not necessary. I do not mean to say that political or social improvements are not necessary but what I mean is this, and I want you to bear it in mind, that they are secondary here, and that religion is primary. The Indian mind is first religious, then anything else. So this is to be strengthened, and how to do it?" Who helps to uphold the world, has religion. How can those who cannot uphold themselves, help to uphold others? Those who truly seek it, will always find the Source of Strength called by many names. The difficulty is that religion is so misunderstood. Both creed and worship may be present without religion. It is sufficient to say here that Dharma is the law of Form. Svadharma is that which upholds one's Form. It is the true nature of the Seed of Race and its manifestations.

Having regard to the past and present circumstances of this country, education given by English teachers or Indians who have been educated by them has produced and now produces some benefits. We must recognise facts. Rightly understood, there is truth in the saying that "What is, is right." This does not mean that what exists in fact to-day is to be approved and continued, but that, until there exists the will and power to effectually change such fact, its past history justifies its present existence. Those who believe in the governance of the world and in Dharma believe that what happens is, under the circumstances, for the best. If India had had in the past the will and power to direct her own education and other affairs, She would have done so, and there would have been neither the need nor opportunity for English control. Education by the English was therefore necessary and what is necessary is beneficial.

But it does not follow that it will always continue to be so, or at least to the same extent as heretofore. India, like other countries is changing, with increasing rapidity. The spirit of the Indian peoples is acquiring power to express itself—that is its Indian self. What the English can teach is of value. But that is not now enough, except for those who are content to be their shadow. What is now needed is an education which, whilst teaching what is of worth in the West, will yet help the Indian people to value their own past contribution to world-culture and to realise their own Indian selves. A conscious and independent self may, and will, assimilate any foreign food which is good for it. The function of the English is to raise this country to life and power. But when so aroused, is this country to merely reflect the light of others, or to be an independent source of light itself? Is the Seed of Race to bear its true fruit? If so, the collaboration of Indian teachers becomes more and more necessary, the aim being in the words of an English writer "Home rule in education" that is, control by Indians over the education to be given to Indians. Abstractedly considered, the claim is in itself so obviously right that it needs no discussion. The real question is a practical one, namely, to what extent it can be given effect to in the best interests of the country. Is there a sufficiency of Indian teachers of the class required, and so forth? Valuable as much of English education is, particularly in its development of a free spirit, it requires to be balanced by an education devised to educe the Sangskâras which are the Seed of Race. This portion of education can *prima facie* be best given by Indian Teachers. But these must be truly Indian themselves and not mere "sedulous apes" of a foreign civilization. If they are, then the English teacher is in every respect preferable. He is original and not a copyist; he has a free and not a copyist's soul. Only a man who is himself free, can bring others up to be free.

Indian culture has a great aesthetic value. But it is not on this ground alone that it is worthy of being maintained. My educational critic, to whom I have already referred, says of the note I submitted to the University Commission that I praise "pretty turbans." I have never done anything of the kind and dislike the word "pretty." And all turbans are not such. But let it pass as a manner of symbolic speech. He cites in this connection the comments (in his own language) of a Japanese journal of the "new school" on Sir Edwin Arnold's appreciation of Japanese scenery, character and art and says "Art forsooth, scenery, and sweetness of disposition. What care we for these? Why did not Sir Edwin praise us for huge industrial enterprises, for commercial talent, for wealth, political sagacity and strong armaments? Of course it is because he could not honestly do so. He has gauged us at our true value and tells us in effect that we are pretty weaklings." He quotes from Basil Halls Chamberlain's "Things Japanese" "Whatever you do, do not praise in the presence of the Japanese of the new school those old quaint and beautiful things Japanese which rouse your most genuine admiration. They *want to be something else than what they have been and still partly are.*"

In so far as these statements imply that the prosperity of Japan is due to her preference of foreign to national ideals, an anonymous correspondent has well pointed out in reply, that notwithstanding Japan's use of such knowledge as is serviceable to Her, she is still Buddhist in religion; instruction is still imparted in Japan through the vernacular; the national philosophy and national literature are still given a prominent place in the school and college curriculum. The Japanese as a whole have kept their traditional religion, traditional morality and traditional culture. What they have done is not to slavishly follow foreign culture, but to engraft such of it as they desired on to the parent stock of their ancestral culture.

The Japanese have not been changed into "a quasi-English breed." They are Japanese first and everything else next. Last but not least, the Japanese govern themselves, and if they take anything from the West it is because as a free people they choose to do so. All this my critic and some others who speak of a "free manhood" conveniently ignore. I am not concerned to defend everything the Japanese have done. There are some who think that they have taken over some things from the West which the latter had better rid itself of. According to Mr. Basil Chamberlain there are, or more probably have been, some Japanese who, like some Indians, "want to be something else than what they have been and still partly are." If by this is meant the abandonment of racial personality, the position is not a true one. If however it is meant that the Racial Soul is to be kept integral, but such of its past products as are really unsuitable for the times are to be cast away and the Racial Soul is to equip itself for the struggle of life to-day, then the position is a true one and none other than that for which I contend. How and in what way this principle should receive practical application is another matter on which there will be difference of opinion. It appears to me that the Japanese are endeavouring to preserve their racial spirit and that, to speak generally, what they have done is with that object. They have recognised that they may be Japanese, and yet take what is of advantage to them from the West. Owing to their acquired capacity to kill successfully with modern weapons they are now recognised as a "civilized" people.

I do think the old life of this country, as also that of Europe prior to the "epoch of the machine," had great aesthetic value. Therefore I love it. I believe that, as has been well said, art is not, in its broadest sense, something that rests outside our ordinary life, to be enjoyed by the initiated or leisured few, but the striving after the Beauty, the Order, and the Fitness of things, to which we all respond in some degree, and which should be the goal of all achievement.

But the aesthetic value of past institutions and practices is not a sufficient ground for preserving them, if they are bad or otherwise unsuitable. Beautiful as they are, they must go if they no longer serve the interests of the people. Other forms, as beautiful as we can make them, must take their place. Let us however be certain, before we abandon what is old and beautiful, that it is really necessary to do so. When saying that India is to evolve on lines of Her own (an obvious truth I should have thought), I am supposed to have meant that She is not in any matter to look to the West for (to use my critic's words) "help to enable her to rise to the height of free manhood." Let me repeat that India may take what She desires from the West or elsewhere, provided that She is not false to Her own Racial Soul.

Moreover I have no doubt that the Government, in giving such education as has been imparted, has done in this matter what it thought best, both in its own interests and in that of this country. The reasons for this conclusion are obvious. As an English Government, it has naturally thought that its own civilization was the best, and that both its own and this country's interests would be served by propagating it. This natural standpoint has been reinforced by a very general attitude assumed by the educated Indians themselves. As many of these have, in the past, depreciated their own culture what is more natural than to assume that if Indian culture is not valued by Indian people, it is without real value? In fact, the English people might have served their material interests better if they had not introduced English education and left the Indian people in cultural seclusion. Only the other day I heard of the statement by a Bengali—"If the English would but leave us our philosophy and religion, we should be content." As a matter of fact, what has been done has acted as a ferment in every sphere of Indian life. The Hand of God is here plainly shown.

For the reasons stated, there may be some who support Indian culture and institutions as tending to the political stability of the country. Further the keeping apart of the eastern and western culture prevents " infection " of the latter by the former. Such calculations have no chance of realization to-day. There are still to be found men, who would have supported the " Orientalists," had they been living at the date of their controversy with the " Anglicists." But it is now too late. I am not concerned with political policy, but to urge that such Education as is given is beneficial to those who receive it. My own view is that education should be continued to be given as regardsEnglish and other western languages, modern science and so forth, though in a better way both as to instruments and subject matter than in the past, but that it should be accompanied by an Indian culture which should be regarded as primary and as designed to foster the Racial Spirit or Seed of Race. If this be done, there will no longer be an attempt to impose one civilization on another, that is, to anglicise the Indian people. They will then remain Indian with all the benefits which a true English education can give them.

But if this result is to be attained, the Indian people must show themselves desirous of it and press for its realization. The old Indian idea that the King is the father of his people was a beautiful one, and has survived amongst some to-day in the notion that the Government and its officers are "Mâ bâp." But the trend of political evolution is away from such ideas. The People and the State tend to become one, and in this country, with every step towards political advancement, the Indian people will become more and more their own "Mâ" and their own "Bâp." The "salt" of Government which they eat will be eventually discovered to be, as in fact it now is, their own salt. Therefore, if they would retain their racial self, they must themselves work to that end. None other can save it for them.

They will gain power (Shakti) to uphold their race and will receive all their desires if they serve their country in the belief that service (Sevâ) of Shri Bhârata is worship (Sevâ) of the Mahâshakti Shrî Bhagavatî who, though appearing in one of Her forms as Bhârata Shakti is not merely a Devî of the Hindus but their *name* for the one Mother of the World.

From this Great power the whole universe comes. In Her womb is the seed of every being in the universe. This universe is not lawless, either as to its parts, or their relation with one another. Each being has its law—the law of its being and the law of its growth. This is its Svadharma. The law or Dharma is not something imposed from without. It is inherent in being, and is in fact the true nature of it. It is the law of form and function. If therefore action (Karma) of any being is not according to the law (Dharma) of its being, that being suffers. Besides the laws common to all human form, there is the law of class (Jâti) or Race. Each member of that race by fulfilling his Dharma is an expression, blissful and success-bringing, of the Creative Idea which has given him birth. He lives in harmony with all, and with strength achieves his purposes. He who in all his acts has devotion to Mahâshakti, on him She, with all Aishvarya, descends (Shaktipâta). Those who want Power must work for it. Those who wish to see India powerful must preserve Her Racial Personality by acting according to Svadharma one of the forms of which is the law of Race.

Swami Vivekânanda was wont to say. "This Âtman cannot be attained by the weak." Who worships Mahâshakti gains power. What is that power? Not something instilled from without. Not the power of some one else, English or other. But the power inherent in the individual and the Race. Worship is given to Mahâshakti in Her form as the Mother-seed of Race, and then in such form She shines.

*19th August, 1919.*

## WORKS BY ARTHUR AVALON ON TANTRA SHASTRA

| | RS. | A. |
|---|---|---|
| **Tantra of the Great Liberation.** (*Mahânirvâna Tantra*). A Translation from the Sanskrit, with Introduction and Commentary by Arthur Avalon ... | 8 | 0 |
| **Hymns to the Goddess.** From the Tantra and other Shâstra and the Stotra of Shangkarâchâryya. With Introduction and Commentary. Translated from the Sanskrit by Arthur and Ellen Avalon ... ... ... | 3 | 0 |
| **Principles of Tantra.** Part I. The Tantratattva of Shrîyukta Shiva Chandra Vidyârnava Bhattâchâryya Mahodaya. Edited with an Introduction and Commentary by Arthur Avalon ... | 8 | 0 |
| **Do do** Part II. With an Introduction by Shrîyukta Barada Kânta Majumdar. Edited by Arthur Avalon ... ... ... | 12 | 0 |
| "**Wave of Bliss**" (*Anandalaharî*) a translation and Commentary by Arthur Avalon ... ... ... | 1 | 8 |
| "**Greatness of Shiva**" (*Mahimnastava of Pushpadânta*) a translation and commentary by Arthur Avalon together with Sanskrit commentary of Jagannâtha Chakravârtti ... ... | 1 | 8 |
| **Origin of the Vajrayana Devatas** by Arthur Avalon ... ... ... | 0 | 8 |

## TANTRIK TEXTS

UNDER GENERAL EDITORSHIP OF

ARTHUR AVALON

| | RS. | A. |
|---|---|---|
| **Vol. I. Tantrabhidhana** *with Bîja-Nighantu and Mudra-Nighantu.*—A Tantrik Dictionary, Edited by Târanâtha Vidyâratna with an Introduction in English by Arthur Avalon ... | 2 | 0 |
| **Vol. II. Shatchakranirupana.**—A work on the six centres of the body by Pûrnânanda Svâmî, with Commentary of Shangkara. *Pâdukâpanchaka*—("Fivefold footstool of the Guru"), with commentary of Kâlîcharana and Notes from the Tîkâ of Vishvanâtha on the Second Patala of Kaivalya Kâlikâ Tantra; with an Introduction in English by Arthur Avalon ... ... | 2 | 0 |
| **Vol. III. Prapanchasara Tantra.**—Edited by Târanâtha Vidyâratna, with an Introduction in English by Arthur Avalon ... ... .. | 3 | 0 |
| **Vol. IV. Kulachudamani Nigama.**—Edited by Girisha Chandra Vedântatîrtha. With an Introduction by Akshaya Kumâra Maitra ... ... | 2 | 0 |
| **Vol. V. Kularnava Tantra.**—Edited by Târanâtha Vidyâratna, with Introduction in English by Arthur Avalon. (*A full translation of this Tantra is in preparation*) ... ... ... ... | 3 | 0 |

RS. A.

**Vol. VI. Kalivilasa Tantra.**—Edited by Pârvati Charana Tarkatîrtha with English Introduction by Arthur Avalon 2 0

**Vol. VII. Shrichakrasambhara.**—A Buddhist Tantra, edited by Kazi Dausamdup with a foreword on the Vajrayâna by Arthur Avalon ...

**Vol. VIII.** First Part **Tantraraja** (*Kâdimata*) Edited by Mahâmahopâdhyâya Lakshmana Shâstri Drâvida ... 3 0

*In the Press*

**Vol. IX.** The Second Part of same is in preparation ... ... ...

**Vol. X. Kamakalavilasa,** a Tantrik Prakarana of the Kashmir School by Punyânanda with Commentary by Anantanâtha ... ... ...

**Vol. XI. Advaitabhavopanishad, Kalyupanishad, Taropanishad, Kaulopanishad.** With Introduction by Arthur Avalon ... ... ...

*To be had of*

LUZAC & CO., LONDON. THACKER SPINK & CO., CALCUTTA. GANESH & CO., MADRAS. TARAPOREWALA & SONS, BOMBAY.